The Greatest Great Nation

Written by Erik Meyers

Illustrated by Anju Chaudhary

This book is dedicated to my Dad, who at the age of 17 forged documents so that he could enlist in the US Navy to fight for his country.

www.erikmeyerswrites.com

Text copyright 2022 by Erik Meyers.

All rights reserved. No part of this publication may be reproduced, stored in a retrieval system, or transmitted in any form by any means, electronic, mechanical, photocopy, recording, or otherwise, without the prior permission of the author, except as provided by USA copyright law.

ISBN: 978-0-578-28417-0

Printed in USA

Of all the great **spots** in the world you could be,
How **amazing** it is that you live here with me,
On this big **rock** that sits between two mighty seas,
As a home for the BRAVE, and a land for the FREE.

Now tell me have you ever thought about this:
What makes this GREAT country as GREAT as it is?

Could it be all the **mountains** and **rivers** and **lakes**,
Or **bald eagles**, **buffaloes**, and **rattlesnakes**?
Perhaps it is **baseball** or **football** for you,
Or that **big bacon burger** off Dad's barbecue?

Well those things ARE great, no argument from me,
But there's something else that I think you should see.
Three things, in fact, in your brain to deposit,
And you need look no further than the COIN in your pocket...

PENNY, nickel, quarter, half dollar or dime,
On every single coin **THREE MOTTOS** you will find.
Three phrases emblazoned to speak from the past
About valuable values we **ALL** should **hold fast**.

So let's **GET TO IT**, no more time to waste,
and eye three ideas that make **AMERICA** so **GREAT**...

E PLURIBUS UNUM is the first thing to **see**,
but unless you know Latin you'll know *not* what it means.
It goes way back to when we'd barely begun –
E pluribus unum means "**Out of many, one**."

MANY we are, and many we've been,
With different backgrounds and colors of skin.
We are MILLIONS of people from all over the globe
Who have made our way here to call this place HOME.

But though we are many, we are also just ONE;
One people UNITED in this race we must run.
So stronger together, there's no place we'd rather be
than this home for the BRAVE, and this land for the FREE.

Look back at that coin and now second you'll find
Why the **Declaration of Independence** was signed.
Longings for LIBERTY burned in those men,
And so **fifty-six** STRONG, they unholstered their pen.

And not just their pens, but their **GUNS** and their **SWORDS**;
As legends of **VALOR**, they were willing to war.
They stood and they fought, handing tyrants defeat,
So that you could be **FREE** and live out your **beliefs**.

There's no place on earth with as free a **foundation**,
Simply no place on earth as **GREAT** as your Nation.
Free to think what you think, and say what you say,
without fear that your **FREEDOM** will be taken away.

There is one more motto, and believe it we must,
That no matter what, IN GOD WE TRUST.
Yes though we do **our** best to keep this country great,
We know to trust in **us** would be a big **mistake**.

People - it's true - can do many *good* things,
But people can also do many *bad* things.
So we need ONE who's bigger and better and greater;
One who can make sure we make it **together**.

This **One** who we need is our GREAT God alone;
His justice and mercy, our true **cornerstone**.
So we take all the **worries** and **fears** and **doubts**
And trust the **Good God** we *can't* do this without.

Well that's all that this little book has to say,
But that's not to say there's not much MORE to say.
I could keep going for pages and pages
And tell you much more for ages and ages.

But these three mottos were a good place to start,
And I hope that you bury them deep in your HEART.
And there in your heart may they burn like an ember,
So in all of your prayers you'll always remember...

That of all the great spots in the world you could be,
How amazing it is that you live here with me,
On this big rock that sits between two mighty seas,
As a home for the BRAVE, and a land for the FREE.

The End.

CPSIA information can be obtained
at www.ICGtesting.com
Printed in the USA
BVHW022219220722
642793BV00002B/124